ONE FLUSH
AT A TIME

ROBERT "DINO" COMER

To order additional copies of this book, contact:
Xlibris
844-714-8691
www.Xlibris.com
Orders@Xlibris.com

ISBN: Softcover   978-1-6641-7877-9
         Hardcover   978-1-6641-7878-6
         EBook   978-1-6641-7876-2

Library of Congress Control Number: 2021911474

Print information available on the last page

Rev. date: 07/21/2022

THIS BOOK IS ONLY MEANT TO BE READ ON THE TOILET
ONE FLUSH PER PAGE

to: _____

from: _____

DEDICATION

I DEDICATE THIS BOOK IN MEMORY OF MY MOTHER
Fannie Julia Thompson Comer,

who gave me the sensitive strength, passion, and vision to fight for good news no matter what disposition I am facing in life.

ACKNOWLEDGMENT

I thank and appreciate Ms. Kara Cardeno, my senior publishing consultant, Mr. Richard Tecson, Author Services Representative, The Design Team and Ms. Rica Caro, publishing consultant with Xlibris Publishing for helping me making One Flush at a Time fun, silly, thought-provoking, and caring to joyfully create for the world!

SPECIAL THANK YOU

Atty. Mandy Kelly and Manager Elyse Fault from the Disability Law Group for making my Hopes a Reality, Dr. Michael Harris, Amy Cynthia, Carey, Taryn, Tonya, Krystal, Sue, and Sharon from Arch Dental for bringing back my Smile, Charles (#flatcharles) and Alice Perchl Swain, Adam Slack, Kate Sunshine Young, Kim Thornlow, Janine Pugh, Quentin Gore, Rusty Brown, Charles and Danielle Irwin, Kimberly Stokley, Brianna Breedlove, Dr. Joy Innis–Johnson, Dr. Teronto Robinson, Shari Lisa Turner, Nita Specht, Stan Best, Sherry B. Botts, Robin K. Edwards, Keara Farmer, Sydney Curley, Bret Smith, Tabitha Sandlin, Eric Brantley, Miranda Lewandoski, Alicia Keating, Paul Johnson, Adam Santiago, Morgan Matthews, Adolfo (AD) Martinez, Martha Keravuori, Mark Sumner Lee, Jim Vidakovich, Tommy and Diane Pierri, Laura Gates and Auntie Janice Habersham and Family.

I've got the Remote . . .

All I need now
is a TV!

I LIKE ~~BIG BUTTS~~ HIGH IQ WOMEN

AND I CAN'T DENY

I WILL NEVER PUT MY HANDS ON A GUN...

BUT IF YOU PUT YOUR HANDS ON ME AGAIN, I'M GOING TO CAULK YOU UP TO AN NRA POSTER!

THE US MILITARY SOLDIER'S INSPIRATIONAL JINGLE

I'VE HEARD EVERY JINGLE
FROM A TO Z.
BUT I'VE NEVER HEARD
A JINGLE ABOUT THE US
MILITARY.
IT'S ONE OF THE GREATEST
ORGANIZATIONS THAT EXIST.
YOU CAN COME IN AS AN
OFFICER OR ENLIST.
THEY'RE BOTH IMPORTANT IN
THIS WORLD.
THEY PROTECT EVERY MAN,
WOMAN, BOY, AND GIRL.
BUT WHO WANTS A WAR,
BATTLE, OR EVEN A FIGHT?
WE ARE HUMAN, AND TO
LIVE, GOD HAS GIVEN US THE
RIGHT. SO THE US MILITARY
OFFERS MORE THAN GUNS,
TANKS, AND GRENADES.
THERE'S COLLEGE, JOB
TRAINING, YOU CAN EVEN
LEARN A TRADE.
SO JOIN THE US MILITARY,
DON'T SETTLE FOR LESS.
THEY WILL EVEN HELP
DEVELOP A TALENT YOU
POSSESS.
SO JOIN THE US MILITARY SO
YOU CAN SEE
THAT IN THE US MILITARY,
YOU DON'T HAVE TO
KILL TO BE FREE!

**The US Military Soldier's
Last Words Jingle**

Oh God, Oh God,
I say to thee,

With a bullet stuck
Deep inside of me.

I've found my home,
Here I'll stay.

Down in this foxhole,
Forever I'll lay.

But before I close my eyes, God,
There is one thing I'd like to express.

Would you explain to the world, God,
How I got into this mess!

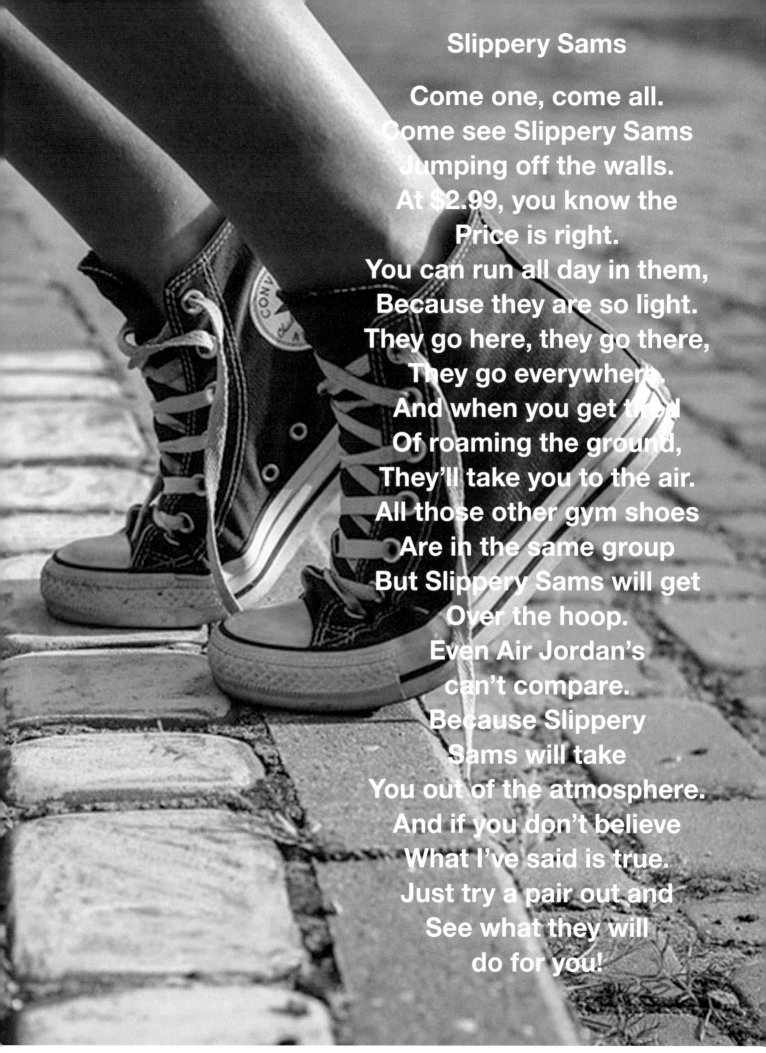

Slippery Sams

Come one, come all.
Come see Slippery Sams
Jumping off the walls.
At $2.99, you know the
Price is right.
You can run all day in them,
Because they are so light.
They go here, they go there,
They go everywhere.
And when you get tired
Of roaming the ground,
They'll take you to the air.
All those other gym shoes
Are in the same group
But Slippery Sams will get
Over the hoop.
Even Air Jordan's
can't compare.
Because Slippery
Sams will take
You out of the atmosphere.
And if you don't believe
What I've said is true.
Just try a pair out and
See what they will
do for you!

Ma, How Do You Talk to People with Respect?

I was just a little fellow when I remembered asking my mother, How you should talk to people with respect? She said, "Dino, don't ever talk over anyone. Don't ever talk down to anyone. Talk to everyone eye to eye! Don't use big words or phrases unnecessarily. That way your heart, soul, spirit, and mind will be understood and appreciated by anyone, no matter what walk of life they come from." I took a moment and looked deep into my mother's eyes, hoping and praying I would understand what she was saying. Hey, I was just a little fellow, remember? But unfortunately, I crawled away more puzzled than before I asked the question. But I must say, after a few little tapping on my little sensitive bottom, I began to understand how to talk to people with respect!

PS: Thanks, Ma, for your tough, passionate, sensitive, and caring heart. Not to mention your firm hand!

THERE IS THIS WOMAN
THAT I LOVE VERY MUCH.

WITH HER SMOOTH, SOFT SKIN
AND HER GENTLE, SWEET TOUCH.

HER HAIR HAS A LUXURIOUS SHINE,

AND WHENEVER I SEE HER, I'M GLAD SHE IS MINE.

SHE IS A VISION OF LOVELINESS,
I LOVE HER WITH TRUTH.

SHE HAS THE ESSENCE OF BEAUTY
AND THE JOY OF YOUTH.

AND AS I SEE HER
UPON CLOSER VIEW.

SHE LOOKS LIKE A SPIRIT,
BUT YET A WOMAN TOO!

HEY, HUMANS,
BEING A FLY ON THE WALL
TO GET SOME GOSSIP
IS NOT ALL THAT IT'S
CRACKED UP TO BE.

IN FACT, THE ALTITUDE
IS KILLING ME!

Here's your lunch, Dad, and please get home before it gets dark. You know howmom worries!

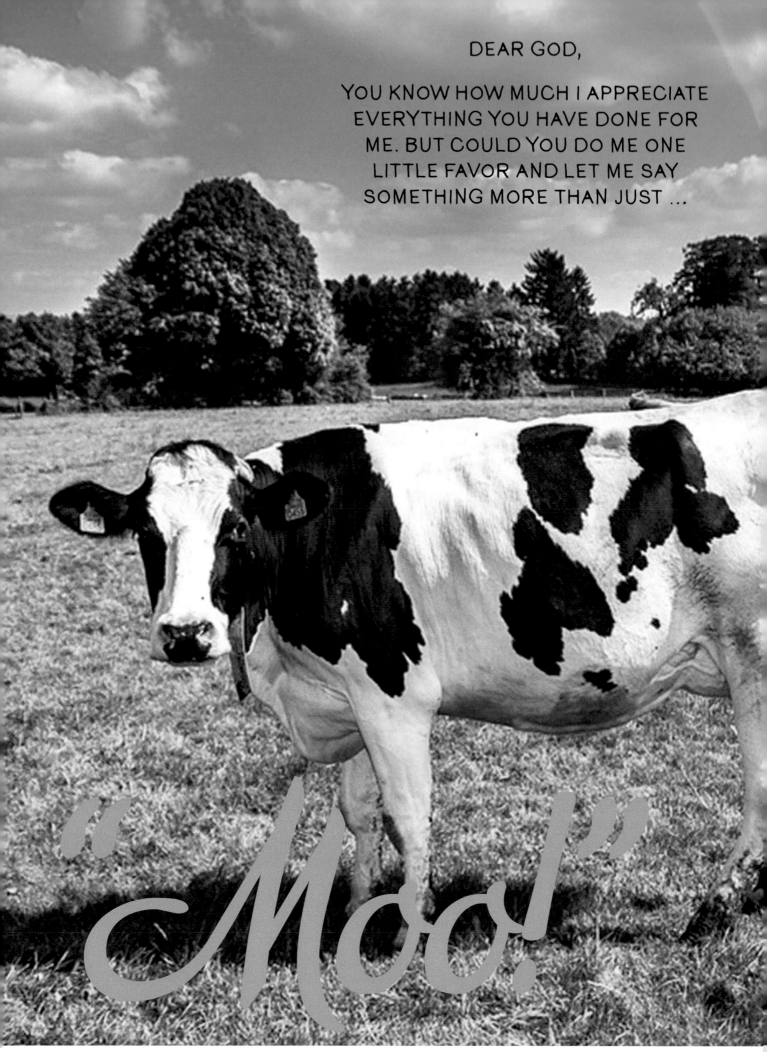

Two men discussing whose grass is greener!

THE GREATEST CRIME
A PERSON CAN COMMIT IS ...

TO STEAL FROM THEMSELVES
AND NOT REALIZING ANYTHING IS MISSING!

Two often, humanity hovers like
a wounded animal, clinging to
life in their poison fence, timidly
seeking and securing their perch.
Afraid to bravely step onto the
side of the fence that they know
deep within their heart is right.

DID YOU GET A NUT? ...

Because I sure got mine!

CAN YOU IMAGINE
HOW MAD A RAT FEELS
WHEN, LOOKING OUT A
BASEMENT WINDOW,

IT SEES IT'S COUSIN, THE
SQUIRREL, RUNNING AROUND
ENJOYING LIFE OUTSIDE?

YOU KNOW IT'S BAD WHEN THE ONLY THING YOU CAN ORDER IN A RESTAURANT IS THE CHECK, AND YOU STILL END UP WASHING DISHES BECAUSE THE CHECK IS TOO EXPENSIVE!

I CAN'T STOP CRYING

BECAUSE TODAY IS SO BEAUTIFUL AND SO FULL OF LIFE!

DO YOU HAVE A TISSUE?

I GOT MY HANDS ON SOME RIBS LAST NIGHT, AND THIS IS HOW IT WENT DOWN!

PEOPLE OF ALL AGES USE SOCIAL MEDIA SO THAT THEY DON'T HAVE TO LOOK PEOPLE IN THE EYES AND COMMUNICATE PERSONALLY!

I've been playing monopoly and chess by myself, and I am losing.

I TOLD A FEMALE POLICE OFFICER

SHE POL
LOOKED
STUNNING!

Then she used a stun gun and stunned me! Aren't you shocked? I sure was!

WHY IS THERE SEPARATE BUT EQUAL FOR BLACKS AND WHITES?

EVERYBODY'S SHIT IS THE SAME!

You Don't have To Be Rich To Be Clean

Because Being Clean is Half The Battle!

I KNOW THOUSANDS OF PEOPLE PROFESSIONALLY, BUT I ONLY HAVE ABOUT 40 REAL AND TRUE FACEBOOK FRIENDS. YOU KNOW, THE KIND OF FRIENDS YOU CAN CALL UP ON THE PHONE, MAIL A LETTER TO, OR GET TOGETHER WHERE YOU CAN HUG OR SHAKE HANDS. I JUST FIND IT HARD TO BELIEVE THAT PEOPLE WHO HAVE HUNDREDS AND THOUSANDS OF FACEBOOK FRIENDS CAN TRULY COMMUNICATE WITH THEM THROUGH REAL AND TRUE FRIENDSHIP LIKE THAT!

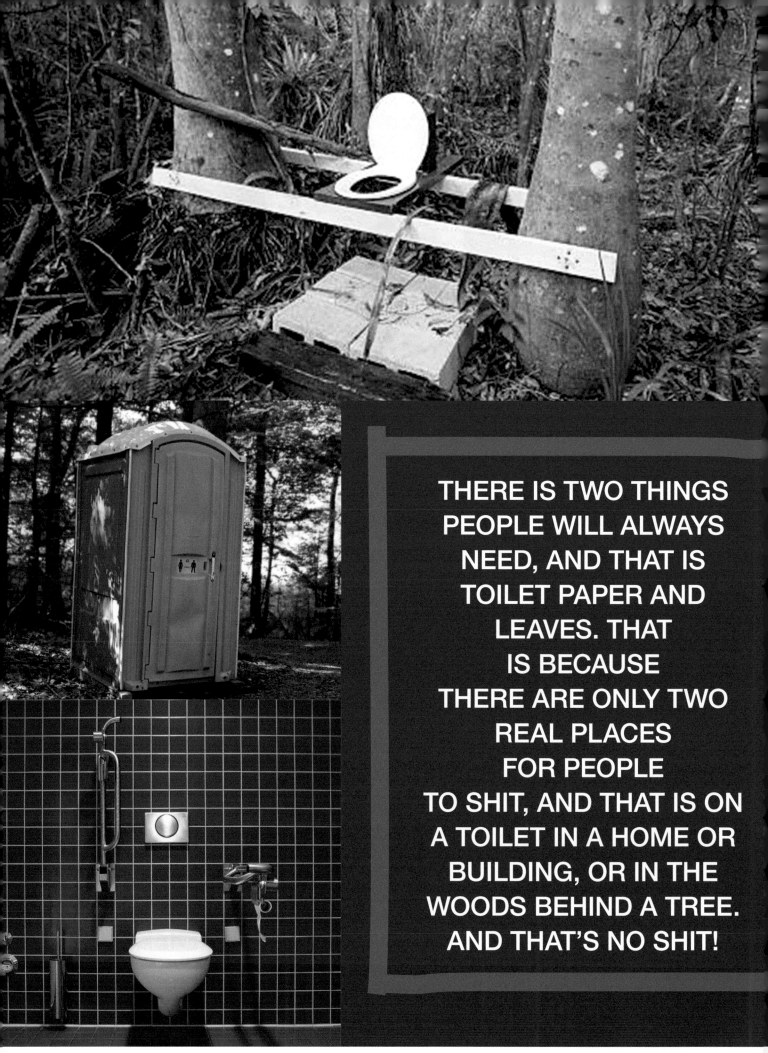

THERE IS TWO THINGS PEOPLE WILL ALWAYS NEED, AND THAT IS TOILET PAPER AND LEAVES. THAT IS BECAUSE THERE ARE ONLY TWO REAL PLACES FOR PEOPLE TO SHIT, AND THAT IS ON A TOILET IN A HOME OR BUILDING, OR IN THE WOODS BEHIND A TREE. AND THAT'S NO SHIT!

LADY: I'M A VIRGIN!

MAN: I'M PROUD OF YOU!

GET MARRIED BEFORE YOU HAVE SEX!

I WAS ON THE BALCONY AND LOOKED DOWN AND SAW A LADY WALKING HER DOG. I SAID, "GOOD MORNING" AND CONTINUED TO SAY, "YOU HAVE A BEAUTIFUL FRIEND"

SHE LOOKED UP AT ME AND SAID, "THANKS FOR COMPLIMENTING MY DOG" I THEN SAID, "OH, I WAS TALKING TO YOUR DOG!" SHE BEGAN BLUSHING AND SAID, "OH, YOU'RE SO SWEET!"

WHEN YOUR FIGHTING FOR THE RIGHT REASONS, IT'S OKAY TO LOSE! BUT DON'T STOP FIGHTING UNTIL YOU WIN! AND THAT'S NO SHIT!

If You Pay Me ...
I'll Work For Free!

Dreams Do Come True, If You Believe In You!

There is one thing people will always need, and that is Toilet Paper. That is because people will always have to Shit!

ABOUT THE AUTHOR

ROBERT "DINO" COMER

AUTHOR, ENTERTAINER, YOUTH ADVOCATE, SOCIAL AND MEDICAL PHILANTHROPIST, AND ARMY VETERAN OF HONORABLE STATUS HAS A DIVERSE, PASSIONATE, AND INNOVATIVE APPROACH TO SUCCESSFUL CREATIVE PRACTICES IN THE FIELD OF PEER MEDIATION AND CONFLICT RESOLUTION. WITH THREE DECADES AS AN EDUCATIONAL VISIONARY, DINO HAS HAD HIS GIFTS AND TALENTS TAPPED INTO BY BEING REQUESTED TO CREATE, CONSULT, WRITE, PRODUCE, DIRECT, LECTURE, AND CONDUCT WORKSHOPS TO A DIVERSE GROUP OF FORTUNE 500 COMPANIES, EDUCATIONAL INSTITUTIONS (KINDERGARTEN TO HIGHER EDUCATION), FEDERAL AND STATE AGENCIES, UNITED STATES ARMY, TELEVISION AND RADIO MEDIA OUTLETS, AND VARIOUS RELIGIOUS OUTLETS.

ALL OF DINO'S BOOKS AND MORE INFORMATION
AND FUN CAN BE FOUND ON ...

WWW.ROBERTDINOCOMERBOOKS.COM

PROCEEDS OF THE SALES OF THIS BOOK WILL BE DONATED
TO HOMELESS VETERANS AND CHILDREN ORGANIZATIONS

Printed in the United States
by Baker & Taylor Publisher Services